How do plants grow?

Louise and Richard Spilsbury

D0316916

young Explorer

www.heinemann.co.uk/library
Visit our website to find out more information about Heinemann Library books.

To order:
 Phone 44 (0) 1865 888066
 Send a fax to 44 (0) 1865 314091
Visit the Heinemann Bookshop at www.heinemann.co.uk/library to browse our catalogue and order online.

First published in Great Britain by Heinemann Library, Halley Court, Jordan Hill, Oxford OX2 8EJ, part of Harcourt Education.
Heinemann is a registered trademark of Harcourt Education Ltd.

© Harcourt Education Ltd 2006
First published in paperback in 2007.
The moral right of the proprietor has been asserted.

Editorial: Kate Bellamy
Design: Jo Hinton-Malivoire and AMR
Illustration: Art Construction
Picture Research: Ruth Blair and Kay Altwegg
Production: Severine Ribierre

Originated by Repro Multi Warna
Printed and bound in China by South China Printing Company

The paper used to print this book comes from sustainable resources

10 digit ISBN 0 431 01804 9 (hardback)
13 digit ISBN 978 0 431 01804 1(hardback)
10 09 08 07 06
10 9 8 7 6 5 4 3 2 1

10 digit ISBN 0 431 01809 X (paperback)
13 digit ISBN 978 0 431 01809 6(paperback)
11 10 09 08 07 06
10 9 8 7 6 5 4 3 2 1

British Library Cataloguing in Publication Data
Splisbury, Louise and Richard
How do plants grow? – (World of plants)
571.8'2

A full catalogue record for this book is available from the British Library.

Acknowledgements
The Publishers would like to thank the following for permission to reproduce photographs:
Corbis pp. **18**, **19** (Patrick Johns), **13** (Lester Lefkowitz), **14**, **26**; FLPA pp. **30** (Minden Pictures: Franz Lanting), **23** (Winfried Wisniewski); Getty Images pp. **4a**, **7**, **21** (Photodisc); Heather Angel p. **5** (Natural Visions); Harcourt Education pp. **28**, **29** (Trevor Clifford); Naturepl.com p. **25** (Andrew Harrington); NHPA pp. **4** (Laurie Campbell), **12**, **27** (Stephen Dalton), **22** (K. Ghani), **10** (Adrian Hepworth); Science Photo Library pp. **5** (Maxine Adcock), **8**, **9**, **11** (Dr Jeremy Burgess), **6** (Adam Hart-Davis), **20** (The Picture Store), **15**, **24**.

Cover photograph of bracken shoots unfurling at the bottom of a beech tree reproduced with permission of Natural Visions/Heather Angel.

Our thanks to Patsy Dyer for her assistance in the preparation of this book.

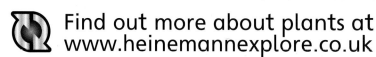
Find out more about plants at
www.heinemannexplore.co.uk

Contents

Words appearing in the text in bold,
like this, are explained in the Glossary.

How do plants grow?

Plants are living things. Most plants start as a **seed**. The seed grows **shoots**. The shoots grow into a young plant. The plant gets bigger and grows flowers.

seed

shoot

When a plant has flowers it can make seeds. The seeds can grow into another new plant!

young plant

flowering plant

Looking at seeds

Inside a **seed** is the part that can grow into a new plant. This is called an **embryo**. There is food inside the seed to keep the embryo alive.

A bean is a seed from a bean plant.

seed

On the outside of the seed is a kind of shell. It is called a seed coat. The seed coat keeps the embryo safe until it is time for it to grow.

An egg shell is a bit like a seed coat. It keeps the baby animal safe until it is ready to be born.

Starting to grow

The first thing to grow out of a **seed** is the **root**. The root grows out of the seed and down into the **soil**.

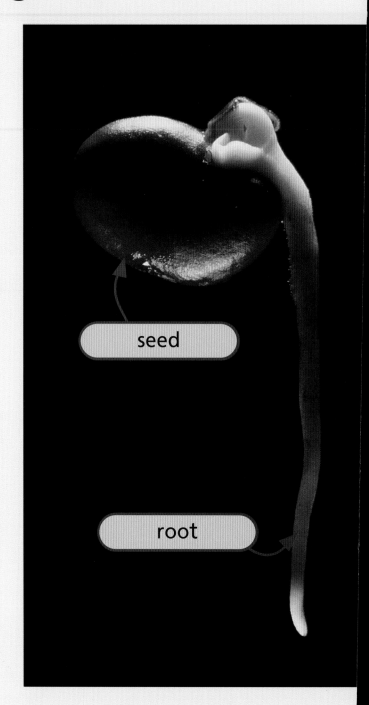

seed

root

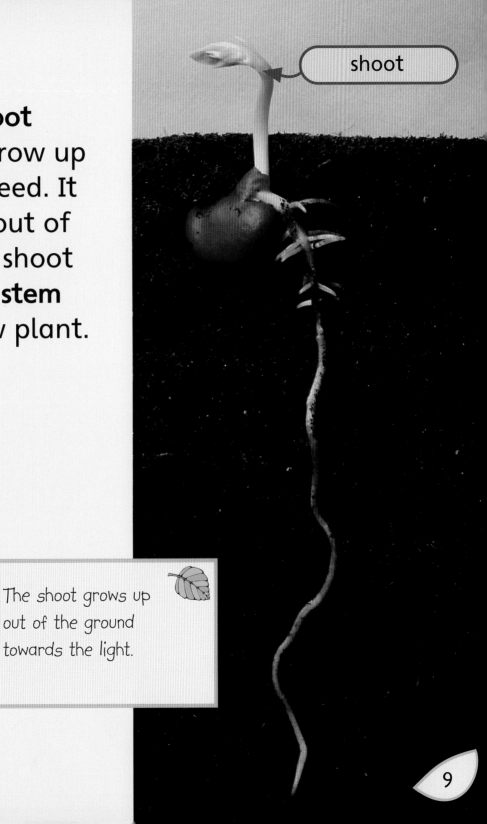

shoot

Then a **shoot** starts to grow up from the seed. It grows up out of the soil. A shoot is the first **stem** of the new plant.

The shoot grows up out of the ground towards the light.

Roots and water

Plants need water like all living things. A plant's **roots** take in water from the **soil**. They also take in **nutrients** that help the plant grow.

Some roots grow long to find water deep in the ground.

Roots grow lots of little root hairs. These hairs help the plant soak up water and nutrients. The water and nutrients move up the root into the **stem**.

root hair

Leaves and light

The **stem** above the ground gets bigger and grows taller. Leaves grow from the stem. They start off as leaf **buds**.

leaf

leaf bud

Leaves swell up and grow out of the leaf buds.

Plants need light to live and grow. Leaves are held up to the light by stems.

Plants arrange their leaves so that they all get some sunlight.

13

Leaves and food

Most living things eat the food they need. Plants make their own food in their leaves. Plants use air, water, and light to make food.

The lines on this leaf are tubes. The tubes carry water to the leaves from the **roots**.

Air is all around us. Leaves have little holes that take in air for the plant. These little holes are called **stomata**.

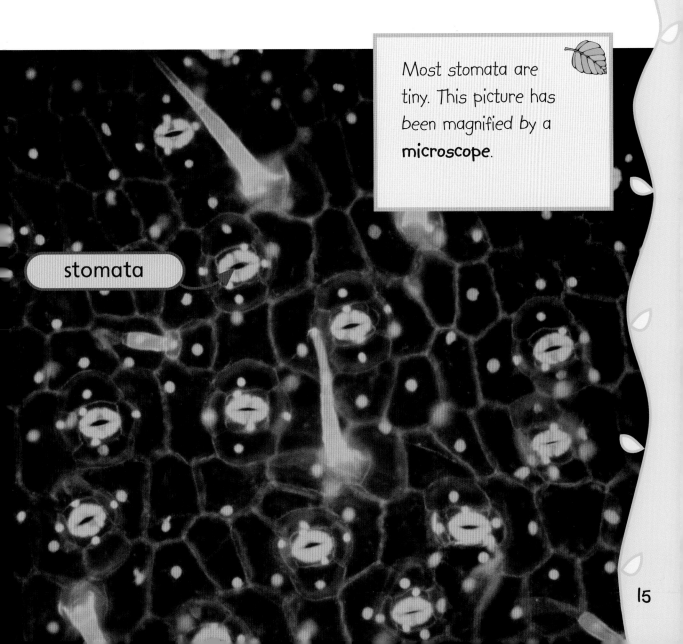

stomata

Most stomata are tiny. This picture has been magnified by a **microscope**.

Making food

Plants use **energy** from sunlight to make their food. Leaves use this energy to turn water and air into sugary food for the plant.

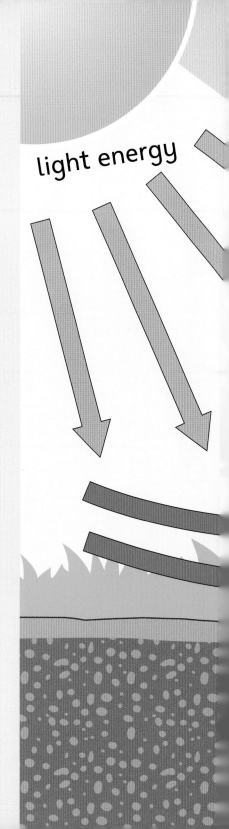

light energy

17

Growing up

Plants use the sugary food to grow bigger. The food moves from the leaves to the rest of the plant. It moves through little tubes.

As plants grow bigger, they grow more leaves.

Tree stems grow very tall and big. They are called **trunks**. Trunks have to be strong to hold up the tree's heavy branches and many leaves.

Growing flowers

Plants change as they grow. Many plants grow flowers in spring and summer when the weather is warm. Some plants grow lots of flowers. Others only grow one.

Different kinds of plants have flowers in different colours, shapes and sizes.

Plants make **seeds** inside their flowers. When the seeds are ready, they fall from the plant. These seeds may grow into new plants.

seed

When do plants stop growing?

All plants keep growing until they die. Some plants only live a few months. They die after they have made flowers and **seeds**.

This plant is dying, but its seeds will grow into new plants next year.

Some plants live for years. Many of these kinds of plant can grow flowers and make seeds every year.

flower

This tree is many years old and still grows flowers.

Storing food

Many plants lose their leaves in winter. This means they cannot make new food. So, they need to store food. Some plants store food in underground **roots** or **bulbs**.

Bulbs can be planted like **seeds**, ready to grow in spring.

In spring the plant uses the stored food to give it **energy** to start growing again. Soon the plant has **stems** and leaves above the ground. Now it can make food again.

Bluebells grow in spring from little bulbs that have been underground all winter.

Changing with the seasons

Many trees and large plants stop growing in autumn and winter. Their leaves change colour and drop off the plant. The plant rests through winter.

Autumn leaves can be yellow, orange, brown, or red.

In spring and summer it is warm and sunny. Many plants that have been resting start to grow again. New plants grow from **seeds** in the ground.

These new leaves are opening in the sunlight and the tree is growing again.

Try it yourself!

Get a sunflower **seed** and have a go at growing your own sunflower.

1. Make a hole in the **soil** and put the seed in it.

2. Cover the seed with more soil and then water it.

Remember to wash your hands after planting the seed!

3. Put the planted seed
   on a windowsill in
   the light.

4. Water the seed
   once a week.

5. Now sit back and
   watch your plant
   grow!

Amazing plants!

Trees are the biggest plants in the world.

Redwood trees, like this one, can grow as tall as a building that is 26 floors high!

 Find out more about plants at www.heinemannexplore.co.uk

Glossary

bud plant part that holds tiny leaves or flowers

bulb underground part that stores food in the winter

embryo part inside a seed that grows into a plant

energy living things need energy to grow and live

microscope scientific instrument that magnifies objects too small for the human eye to see

nutrient substance that helps living things grow

root plant part that grows underground

seed plant part that contains an embryo, which can grow into a new plant one day

shoot first stem and leaves of a plant

soil earth that plants can grow in

stem plant part that holds up leaves and flowers

stomata tiny holes on a leaf that take in air for the plant

trunk large woody stem of a tree

More books to read

Nature's Patterns: Plant Life Cycle, Anita Ganeri (Heinemann Library, 2004)

Read and Learn: Life cycles: Broad Bean (Louise Spilsbury, 2003)

Index